THE BRUSHES *of* LIFE

THE BRUSHES *of* LIFE

DONALD E. SHEPPARD

XULON PRESS

Xulon Press
2301 Lucien Way #415
Maitland, FL 32751
407.339.4217
www.xulonpress.com

Paperback ISBN-13: 978-1-66283-493-6
Ebook ISBN-13: 978-1-66283-685-5

This book is dedicated to my wife Sarah, our daughter Donarah, and the memory of my parents: The late Bishop Elbert Lee Sheppard, Sr. and the late Mrs. Floria Chavers Sheppard

TABLE OF CONTENT

Preface

I recently attended a concert in St. Louis, Missouri, one thousand miles away from my home. I didn't travel there especially for the concert. I was attending a church convention, and the tour happened to be in that city. I had a rare chance to see this group, a favorite of mine as far back as my college days. The group, Commissioned, was an all-male group who were close to my age. Now with gray hair and slower movement, they had gotten back together for a reunion concert. I reeled with joy, basking in the familiar sounds and lyrics from the 1980s. These songs, which I would play repeatedly, tapped into my life stories, challenges, and experiences. At the same time, they encouraged me to accomplish my goals and keep my faith strong. At the reunion concert, I was ecstatic; I learned a lot about the group's history and heard of their humble start. I realized something after later reflecting on the words of the founder: his journey started as an expression, a musical means to document ideas, and a couple of musicians getting together with the same language to speak their truths. This musical language was like a brush through which the content of their souls would flow. It would flow to the canvas of vinyl records and tapes, which allowed its beauty to be on display for all to see. Not only was this "brush" a means by which I could see their souls, but a means by which I could use these songs to express myself to others.

Let me explain what I mean about this brush of mine. You would have to follow me back to the church. You see, the career I was pursuing was in the visual arts; however, I had a side interest in gospel music, and it would often manifest itself in organ playing, singing, and teaching songs to the church choir. Every time I heard a good song on the radio, I would put a tape in, press record, and prepare it for the next rehearsal. I became preoccupied with good songs, and they became the content of my soul. Teaching them and hearing the choir sing them became my brush and masterpiece. I would get so excited about Commissioned songs that I would teach them to the youth in my church. There, young people were eager to find something worthwhile to do and would "eat it up." The brushes of the band Commissioned were producing masterpieces that were inspirational enough to activate the brushes of music within me. I, in turn, utilized my brushes to make expressions through groups of young people in my church.

This idea of a brush is a tangible yet a metaphoric illustration of a reality in all of us. My theory is: we all have a brush (or brushes) that carry our thoughts to an expression, thereby enabling us to exhibit what is within us. I further believe that awareness of this is powerful, and identifying these brushes and their uses will render us more expressive, less anxious, and with a greater feeling of productivity. We can start by clarifying what is the general content of this book.

Chapter 1

THIS BOOK IS NOT ABOUT ART.

I have to do something (and I hope I don't disappoint anyone); I have to begin with a disclaimer and say right away that this book is not necessarily about art. You may hear terms associated with the visual arts, but the concept is far broader and is simply unlimited in its application to other subjects, disciplines, and categories. Therefore, a brush can refer to a hobby, a propensity toward technology, comedy, a sport, a physical attribute, writing, speaking, or even a personality. Get this: a brush can be anything (and here it is) that serves as a tool for your expression. I can further explain in the next chapter, but for now, let us deprogram our schemas and make room for what else a brush may look like.

I often explain to my middle school art students what "schema" is. It is like a file folder we keep in our brains. In the folder, we have saved images of particular items according to our experiences. Therefore, schema is the images we already have saved in our minds when we think of concepts. For example, let's take the instance of a brush. We already have an image in our minds. Let us try this together: go into that file folder labeled "brush." That's right, open it up. Do you see the image? A handle with a metal part near the top with bristles coming out? What color is your brush? Is it black? Brown? Are the bristles soft and tapered to a point? On the other hand, is there a square tip good for ninety-degree angles? Maybe your brush is big enough to paint a room in the house or small enough to paint the hairs on a cat's back. Whatever you find in your schema, it (I dare to say) somewhat looks similar to the image on the front of this book. Brushes, brushes, brushes… enough! Now let us start deprogramming.

*Brushes, rushes, rus es, us es, s s, s. . .*GONE!

Now let us go back and add other possibilities in our "brush folder." Doctor, rapper, hair stylist, event planner, jogger, barber, pilot, clean-up crew, and the list goes on. I hope by now there are other images in your schema folder for brushes.

For example, since I am a minister, one of the brushes I use is a sermon. A sermon is a means by which I can convey a thought and exhibit a concept. A sermon sometimes develops like a painting. It sometimes develops over weeks. A thought here and a scripture there that seem to relate to an overarching theme. These thoughts merit more research, which informs what I already know. Finally, every color is applied carefully to paint a picture that is digestible and communicates a message. This message becomes a masterpiece. At the same time, performing the sermon becomes the brush and the means by which I can effectively express my soul.

Therefore, possibilities are plentiful when thinking about brushes. We can unlock our limited images and welcome a multiplicity of ways in which we express ourselves. Though a brush is normally associated with art supplies, this book is about much more. In fact, I consider this book itself a brush—a means by which we talk about brushes. Let us continue to talk and define the brush more in the next chapter.

Chapter 2

THE BRUSH

I said this book is not about art. However, I need a bit of art to make my next point. Allow me to get artsy just for a moment, and I will be right back. Come with me as we go to the beginning of the sixteenth century, around 1503, where a young man by the name of Leonardo da Vinci is painting a portrait of a woman named Lisa. I understand it took him about three years to complete it. Well, not really "complete" it, because Lisa never got it. Several factors have made this portrait well-known, including Leonardo's use of atmospheric perspective, the question of whether or not Mona Lisa is smiling, and the fact that it was stolen for a while in the early 1900s. Whatever you thought of it and regardless of who introduced it to you, it is one of the most reproduced images in the history of painting. We know it when we see it, and the image is so prevalent my mother-in-love has a print of it on her dining room wall.

Now, imagine for a moment Leonardo painting it. What did he use? How did he blend the lights and darks that differentiate her chin from her neck? He must have used some instrument to get the paint on the canvas. Hmmm…what could that be? Ah, you guessed it…brush! A brush that was an instrument, a means by which the paint moved to the canvas and became the image it was. Now, the point I want to make is this: the brush is not the painting, and the painting is not the brush. The painting is that manifestation of the image Leonardo wanted to move from his mind to the world. The painting is that image so intriguing that other painters like Marcel Duchamp could not resist altering it. However, the brush was only the means to make it happen.

This therefore illustrates an important concept. The brush is an avenue and not necessarily the destination. It allows us to say something yet is not as important as what we say. In fact, different brushes or tools could have said the same thing and yielded the same basic results. What if Leonardo did the

Mona Lisa with cotton balls or an electronic drawing program, or an airbrush? The *Mona Lisa* would still be the *Mona Lisa* (well, maybe with a slightly different visual technique.)

Okay, we are leaving the art world and coming back to a broader reality. The main thing is the main thing. A brush can get you there. I saw recently that a couple of teenagers went viral when they posted themselves giving clothes to a special classmate who had been bullied (TheEllenShow, 2019). This was a self-correcting effort because the teens, Kristopher and Antwain, had previously participated in making fun of their classmate Michael. After reflecting, they wanted to apologize and give the student new clothes. The Big Picture here was to show how people should treat others. The teens used the brush of their influence as football players to get the message across that people should treat one another nicely. After their video went viral, Ellen DeGeneres invited them to her show. Not only did they get to tell their story, but also, Will Smith made a surprise appearance and showered them with new clothes and gifts. Another company, Shutterfly, collaborated with Ellen and gave the teens $10,000 each. The masterpiece in the story is the message of being kind. The teens used their platform (or brushes) as football players to say, "Be kind." Ellen used her brush as a talk show host to say, "Be kind." Will Smith used his brush as an actor to say, "Be kind." The company Shutterfly used its brush as an organization to say, "Be kind." They all used their brushes, and they all ended with the same important message.

We can distinguish the brush from the most important part. It is the means or tool by which we get there.

Chapter 3

WORKING YOUR BRUSH

So...what will you do with your brush? Before answering this question, listen to a story I heard.

There once was a man who ascended the highest levels of his social and academic circles. He had a reputation of being straight forward with his convictions. As a young man, he had seen his mentors rid the community of "troublemakers." One day, he witnessed his elders forcing a man out of the city and murdering him. This young man participated by holding the coats of the murderers. As this young man grew older, he continued the murderous trend he had seen. He was determined to get rid of those who did not fit his way of thinking. He was actually, one day, on his way to kill some "aggravating people" when suddenly, he saw a light. It was so blinding, he lost control of his vehicle, was ejected, and ended on the ground. As he laid there, he had an epiphany. It was as if God was talking to him, encouraging him to find a better way. From that day forward, he was a changed man. When he recovered from the accident, he wanted to help the very people he had been hurting. It took a while for people to see that he was a changed man.

Soon he began to be an advocate for the very ones he had tried to eliminate. He published many writings that became textbook-like instructions for this new way of life. The person I am speaking of is a man by the name of Paul. Paul the apostle is a well-known biblical personality who wrote thirteen of the sixty-six books of the Bible (20 percent of the Bible). The same Paul who used his energy to hurt people later used his energy to build people. Paul is a classic example of brushwork. We have the choice to work our brushes toward destruction or to work our brushes toward construction.

Paul's brushes were his zealous personality, his wit/intelligence, and his ability to influence. He used his brushes negatively to destroy people. However, when he had a change of heart, he used the same brushes to put "broken people" together.

Whatever our brushes, they can always use some stirring into optimism. Maximize the use of your brush by choosing to look for the best, wash out negative thoughts, and build people, rather than tear them down. Work your talents, resources, expertise, and tools toward hope and healing. There is enough destruction out there already. You can win with a good attitude. Sometimes, the smallest of brushes will make the biggest of differences. Work it well.

Chapter 4

THE BIG PICTURE

A museum visitor captured a moment of a two-year-old girl staring at a painting of Michelle Obama while the little girl's mother was trying to get her attention (Harris, 2018.) The toddler was lost in the painting, and the photo went viral. Eventually, little Parker Curry got to not only meet Michelle Obama but be the guest on numerous television shows. She was also the featured star in her own book at age four. Her fascination with the museum painting encapsulates the power art can have on the observer. The experience can vary. The painting may prompt one to stare in admiration or cause one to think reflectively. Some art makes a social justice statement and inspires one to action. Whatever the reaction and response to art, "The Big Picture" is the common item of focus. The Big Picture is the intent of the artist, the framed phenomenon, and the item displaying the final statement. Artist Amy Sherald possibly used several brushes to paint the patterns in Michelle Obama's long dress and modulated the lights to dark in the smooth finish of her sleeveless arms. However, the brushes were not as significant as the final piece – The Big Picture that caused little Parker Curry to stare in awe.

The Big Picture is significant when realizing the brushes of life. Our brushes are tools to get us to the important things—the things that matter and the end products. Examples of The Big Picture may be a sense of community, an innovative solution, the love of kindred, laughter in the kitchen (see chapter 10), or the rescue of someone in danger. The Big Picture brings purpose to brushes and brings meaning to their existence.

Furthermore, having a big picture in mind brings clarity to the process and production of the painting. For this reason, it is useful to have big pictures in mind so that our brushes can operate. These could be simple things that we take for granted but are really masterpieces: such as freedom, harmony, balance, unity, encouragement, and kindness. Understanding focus assists in prioritizing what is important. For example, football players use their brushes of athletic talent to play a rival game. One team loses while the other wins. However, The Big Picture is a spirit of cooperation that contributes to the economic success of participating hosts and the byproduct of healthy players.

We can further look at "Big Pictures" in terms of goals. Every artist has a goal in mind that guides his/her painting tools to do what he/she does. Even Jackson Pollock and the abstract expressionists had concepts in mind that guided them. Likewise, when we use our life brushes, we benefit from having goals that bring focus and purpose. We should be careful with our goals and be sure they are not too vain, self-centered, or vindictive. We should consult our God, the Creator of our brushes, so that we can properly set goals that will make full use of our talents.

It is also important to realize that goals (or big pictures) can be short range or long range. Long-range goals are the things we envision for the future: owning a home, getting a degree, or winning a marathon. The short-range goals are the things we do to get to the long-range goals. For example, if owning a home is our long-range goal, a short-range goal could be saving for a down payment, choosing a realtor, or devoting an hour a day to research. Though we can consider any goal "a big picture," it is easy to characterize long-range goals as "The Big Picture" and short-range goals as "pieces of the puzzle." We can be just as happy with the puzzle pieces as we are with the total picture. It is okay to use our brushes to do the little things: coach a Little League team, organize a neighborhood clean-up day, and take food to a grieving family. Soon, the puzzle will start coming together. The Big Picture of "making a difference in the community" will soon become evident.

This is true in the case of Greg Grady, a talented basketball star. Grady played for Florida State University from 1972 to 1976. His talent landed him the opportunity to play with the French Federation for five years. When Grady came back to Tallahassee, Florida, he started doing little things in his community to give back. He coached Little League. At the neighborhood recreation center, he started providing after-school activities for energetic kids. He organized dances and tournaments to keep idle hands busy and eased the minds of hard-working parents (Dobson, 2017). Bit by bit and puzzle piece at a time, he utilized his brush (his expertise and time) to allow youth to mature and become productive and appreciative citizens. After thirty-three years, leaders in the community organized and named the gymnasium after him. The gym now reflects The Big Picture of "making a difference" as it exhibits it new name, The Greg Grady Gymnasium. Grady used his brush to make incremental gains that would result in a big picture of positive change. What an inspiration!

Chapter 5

The Medium

So, you believe me, right, when I say, "this book is not about art." You believe me? Well, if you find it hard to believe, I'm going to give you more reason to doubt in this chapter. We are using tools and terms familiar to artists. However, the concepts are applicable to any professions, endeavors, or accomplishments in life's journey. Just keep that in mind while we look at another term on the art vocabulary list: medium.

The medium is the "stuff" one uses to make his/her art. Often, when artists meet, greet, and conversation ensues, it is not readily apparent what type of art one does. The question arises during the conversation like this: "Oh, you're an artist too? What medium?" The response may be any of the following: oils, acrylics, color pencils, clay and ceramics, pastels, stone, fiber, bronze, glass, or mixed media. By the way, "media" is the plural form of "medium."

If I were to use the word media, immediately my students would think I was speaking of the news or any form of social media. I would have to convince them that I used media "before media was cool." The media I used filled my brush and spread across my canvas to make beautiful art. It was the bridge between the brush and the picture. The medium (or the paint in the case of a painting) is not the brush (the tool) but the substance that yields itself to the outcome. The medium is at one with the brush until it allows itself to become the messenger (and the message) of The Big Picture.

When thinking about the medium, one can remember that a medium is in the middle. It is not large nor small, rare nor well-done, high nor low, hot nor cold. It is in between, the connector, the bridge and the means. Because it is in harmony with the brush, it is the link to what a brush can do for a big picture. Look at the chart to see the possible relationships between the brush, the paint (medium), and the picture. Then try coming up with a few of your own.

Possible Brushes. Medium, and Big Picture Relationships

The Brush	The Medium	The Picture
Cook	Food	Full Course Meal
Mother figure	Good Advice	Feeling of Security
Car Mechanic	Repair tools, parts, and knowledge	Functional Transportation
Fiction Writer	Words	Wonders of Imagination
Comedian	Interpretation and Presentation	Lifting With Laughter
Gymnast	Body movements	Physical Expression
Antique Collector	Relics of the past	Preservation
Mayor	City Departments	City Character
Gardner	Seeds, Soils, and Plants	Bloom and Harvest
Truck Driver	Mobile Goods	Delivery
Good Student	Curriculum	Academic Inspiration
Carpenter	Building Materials and tools	A building or products
Florist	Flowers	Flower arrangement/decor
Babysitter	Baby and setting	Parents taking a break

Chapter 6

THE BRUSH, SOCIALIZATION, AND CULTURE

Vincent Van Gogh, a well-known artist of the nineteenth century, only lived to age thirty-seven. During his brief art career, he only sold one painting. However, years after his death, the art world has come to appreciate his contribution to post-impressionism. Many today hail him as a genius, even though his mental health challenges are evident in the infamous act of him cutting off his ear. We can thank his sister-in-law for gathering and preserving his many works we enjoy today. During Vincent's lifetime, he tried several other careers. In addition to being a minister for a short time, he worked as an art dealer. He only got into this profession because he had an uncle in the business. When young Vincent's parents sent him to stay with his uncle, he assimilated into his environment and picked up the profession (Callan, 1997).

Like Vincent, we all live within an environment, a set of circumstances, and a context, regardless of the potentials inside us. This may explain why there are children who take on the trade of their parents and sustain the life of a business over several generations. What we experience in our surroundings has a profound effect on us and the brushes we choose in life. Our socialization and cultures often steer us into our way of doing things, how we communicate, and what is meaningful to us.

Ian Robertson (1977) defines socialization as "the process of social interaction through which people acquire personality and learn the way of life of their society" (p. 568). If you grew up in an Italian house where the kitchen was central and you can remember Grandmother clanging pots while the aroma of sauce lingered in the air, you will likely learn some of the recipes you enjoyed as a child. It is no wonder that different restaurants of specific cultural foods emerge throughout our neighborhoods. For any given "eat-out" meal, we can choose Italian, Chinese, Mexican, soul food, or Caribbean (to name a few). The reality is cultural brushes have been passed down through generations enough so that many can enjoy The Big Picture of a great night out.

According to Robertson, there are at least four ways socialization takes place: through family, through schools, through peers, and through mass media. Families usually get the first opportunity to influence us. Family members may even encourage us to follow our dreams and do what no other family member has done. Schools are more formal, and we learn things, not only intentionally but unintentionally as well. We learn to heed to authority, take turns, be polite, and work as a team in our schools. Our friends and peers bring a very influential element to our socialization. We explore, interact, and progress on a basis of equality. We sometimes find our friends based on the "brushes" we enjoy and have in common. We make friends on the track team, chess club, theatre class, or calculus honors class. We sometimes make lifelong friends doing the things we want to do.

In addition, mass media has made peer associations all the more possible. Through social media, it is easy to share ideas across the world in a matter of seconds. This proved true in the aftermath of the Stoneman Douglas tragedy. After seventeen high school students and staff members died in a mass shooting in Parkland, Florida, students took on the seemingly impossible task of changes in gun legislation. Even after years of school shootings, the pattern of non-progress remained the same. However, these students used their influence (brushes) through the powerful medium (paint) of social media. In a matter of weeks, they influenced hundreds to march in Florida's capital and eventually thousands around the world (Call, 2018). Florida responded to The Big Picture by passing some legislation. Social media is undoubtedly a key element in the influence and socialization of our generation. Used responsibly, it can play a major part in movements toward improvement and social justice.

Social media also enables various cultures to interact. Culture, according to Robertson, is "all the shared products of human society, comprising its total way of life" (p. 562). In my opinion, cultural members should not go silent due to ethnocentric scoffers who make light of the cultural members' convictions. My thought is this: do what you do and do it well, and people will come looking for you. I remember as a little boy sitting around with my twin brother waiting for my mother in Mrs. Aggie's house. Aggie Cook (we called her Sister

Cook) did hair as a side job. She only had a little space in her living room, but people came from all over town to get their hair done. These were the days when the hair stylist would put a curling iron over a blazing stove, fill a divided portion of hair with grease, and sizzle it to a rolled-up curl tight as a tire. That roll of hair was so set, it would not move if you blew it. Sister Cook would be talking, praying, testifying, comforting, and instructing, all while she did hair…and she was good! She was so good that eventually, her husband added a room to their house, and she had her own space. She was so good, people came and found her, and she quickly filled her new beauty parlor. When she passed away suddenly, the community was shaken. It took my mother a while to find someone she could trust with her hair. People came from miles and miles to honor Sister Cook. She is proof that if you do what you do well, your gift will make room for you. Her brush was her hair dressing skills, but The Big Picture was the fact that she encouraged many lives along the way.

I therefore encourage all brush holders to stand strong no matter where you are, what your cultural heritage is, what socialization looks like for you, or what your normal is. Like Sister Cook, do what you do well, and people will come looking for you. Take pride in your heritage; gravitate to what is good, wholesome, and positive. Spit the "bones" out and anything negative that is not worth perpetuating. Be true to your experiences, and your "brushes" will merit appreciation.

Finally, there is no need to feel like cultural brushes isolate us from the rest of society. When we embrace our heritage, this gives us a perspective and a voice by which we interact with other cultures. Brushes may stem from different geographical, philosophical, and ceremonial norms. However, The Big Pictures they make often have common outcomes of values, survival, and balance. Variations in brushes provide an opportunity to come together in a mural of mutual understanding.

The ways our families, friends, schools, and environments have socialized us may become the immediate tools available to us for expressions. This is normal, and one should consider it useful. Exploring our cultural brushes will likely bring authentication to our big pictures.

Chapter 7

BRUSHES, NEEDS, AND OTHER THEORIES

How necessary is it to have a brush in life? Can we get by with no "tools"—no way to express ourselves? What if we had potential in us, but we had no way to get it out? One of the most memorable points in Helen Keller's autobiography to me is the moment she learned how to spell "water" in sign language. She had been defiant, rude, stubborn, and frustrated until she discovered the tool of words to express herself and understand what her teacher was expressing to her. For her, words were brushes by which she could communicate to the world and realize her never-before-seen potential.

Like Helen, I wonder if the world puts the talented aside too soon before they find the brush that best communicates their souls' big picture. Where there is no brush, there is a higher likelihood of frustration, defiance, explosion, and acting out. As an educator, I understand how not to give up on the uninterested students. By understanding learning styles, using current events, noting child development stages, incorporating cooperative learning techniques, and other strategies, one can find that brush that will unlock the flow of expression. Students need that flow in order to grow. Moreover, when they become adults, the need continues.

There is therefore a need for brushes in life's journeying. Let's explore the need for brushing through the context of Abraham Maslow's hierarchy of needs (1943). In 1938, Maslow argued that people have at least five levels of need. On the first level, the needs are physical. Examples include air, water, food, and things we need to survive. On level two, there is the need for safety. This includes shelter, protection, and security. On level three, Maslow argued that people need love and a sense of belonging. Level four is a need for self-esteem and the need to be respected and recognized. Finally, the fifth level is the need to realize potential, be creative, and be all one can be. These levels of needs are set up in a pyramid model as each level is dependent upon the other (level one needs must be satisfied before level two needs, level two needs must be satisfied before level three needs, and so on.)

If we look at Maslow's law in terms of our need for brushing, we may find our brushing somewhere on levels three, four and five. On level three, our need to belong and "fit in" can lead to our preference of expression. A dad who loves baseball may often take his son to baseball games and prompt the development of the same appreciation for baseball in his kid. A sense of belonging may inspire us to be a part of a group or community with like passions. In level four of the pyramid, the need for respect may develop into a profession and expertise in the field of one's choice. Possibly, a graphic emblem may emerge and show the existence of one's interest (or brush)—a plumber, a YouTuber, a realtor, or a motivational speaker. We *need* these brushes to express our souls and move about in relation to our surroundings. As we do, we respect and we gain respect from others.

Finally, level five on the pyramid is about self-actualization. We have a need to realize everything we could possibly be and fulfill everything we could possibly dream. Level five gives cause to the need for brushes and reaches into The Big Picture. We need brushes so we can be what we can be. Being what we can be is why we cannot "shut up and dribble."

Shut up and dribble? This statement is the "gift" of a journalist, Laura Ingraham. She made this comment in 2019 after popular basketball player LeBron James dared to share his opinion concerning a political issue. She argued that he should just stick with his talent (levels three and four) and stop there. However, Mr. James recognized a bigger picture of influencing many who would listen to his words and be affected by his leadership. He could not (and did not) hold his peace and passively play basketball (shut up and dribble). He continued sharing his opinions and extending his dribbling to bigger pictures, including building a school for disadvantaged youth and providing scholarships. I suspect that Mr. James *needed* to do these actions in order to satisfy his soul.

Steve Harvey calls this level of need a "calling" or a "gift." He makes a distinction between a talent and a gift (The Official Steve Harvey, 2018). He says one's talent is something that one can do well. However, one's gift is what one is called to do—it is the purpose for being. Harvey argues that a gift is the thing one does best with the least amount of effort.

We can parallel his terms to those we used in this book. The talent is the brush (tool or instrument) by which we fulfill our calling (The Big Picture.) Harvey further speaks of passion and distinguishes it from a gift. Harvey, however, encourages people to follow their gifting. There will be more on passion in chapter ten. For now, passion fits well with Maslow's needs theory, and often, those who have a passion for an interest feel a need to pursue that interest. This is what Irving Stone suggested in his book *The Agony and the Ecstasy* (1961), when he wrote, "One *should* not become an *artist because he can*, but *because he must. It* is only *for* those who would be miserable without *it*" (p. 84).

The need and propensity for the arts is what led to Howard Gardner's research on cognitive development and the emerging theory of multiple intelligence (1985). Gardner found that there were other categories of genius and proficiencies outside of mathematics and science. Other areas once thought as only emotional were cognitive as well. Gardner's theory of multiple intelligence initially included seven categories: (1) linguistic intelligence (lawyers, speakers, writers, and poets); (2) logical-mathematical (mathematicians, logicians, and scientists); (3) musical intelligence (musicians, performers, composers);

(4) bodily-kinesthetic intelligence (dancers, actors, athletes; also craftspeople, surgeons, and mechanics); (5) spatial intelligence (navigators, pilots; also sculptors, surgeons, chess players, graphic artists, and architects); (6) interpersonal intelligence (salespeople, teachers, clinicians, religious leaders, political leaders, and actors); and (7) intrapersonal (the capacity to understand oneself, including desires, fears, and capacities.) Gardner later added three other areas of intelligence: naturalist (biologists and environmentalists), spiritualist (religion, mysticism, or transcendence), and existential intelligence (the ability to locate oneself with respect to the cosmos).

Okay, all those areas of intelligence provide plenty to explore. The essential point is: there are multiple areas by which one may express himself/herself. These are brushes serving as tools for making our marks in the world. The marks get us to masterpieces and the meaningful big pictures of importance.

Maslow's hierarchy of needs

Chapter 8

THE BRUSH (TOOL) OF
DETERMINATION

Early in my art career, I heard about the story of Joni Eareckson Tada. As a teenager, Joni experienced a devastating accident (Tada, 2001). Her active and vibrant lifestyle changed suddenly when she dove into shallow water and broke her neck. She tells of the immediate loss of sensation in the majority of her body. She was and remains paralyzed from her neck down. After many years of emotional turmoil, Joni found a new way to express herself by holding a brush with her teeth. Her determination and refusal to give up on life propelled her into the production of some incredible paintings. Joni's brush truly became a brush of life as she allowed creativity to flow through the untraditional method of her mouth in order to communicate ideas and master big pictures.

Joni's story is a great illustration of the "brush of determination." This brush is seemingly available as a companion to all brushes and sometimes supersedes the limitations of brushes. In other words, the brush of determination is like a wild card: it goes with every color, number, or category to go on and win the game. In Joni's story, one of her brushes was likely her love for swimming. It was a means by which she expressed herself. However, when that brush was no longer available, she had another brush inside of her (or accompanying her) that would not stop. That brush was the brush of determination. Determination led her to the brush of painting with her mouth. Determination further helped her utilize the brush of painting to continue life, get married, write books, and encourage others.

Determination is a strong tool. It will sustain the challenged until other means for survival emerge. Often times, great masterpieces are realized through determination. By determination, we expand technology, increase innovation, invent lifesaving devices, develop vaccines, and create new possibilities. We also get through adverse situations like incarcerations, tragedies, abuse, setbacks, and loss.

As a Christian, I find determination to be very biblical. Most ministers I know can quickly structure a sermon on determination by referencing subjects like Israel crossing the Red Sea in Exodus 14, the unjust judge of Luke 18, the ill woman who was determined to touch the hem of Jesus's garment, and Jesus Himself enduring His death on the cross. The teachings of Jesus encourage followers to believe enough to move forward with determination. It is then that new avenues emerge and the seemingly impossible becomes possible.

Antonio Davis also discovered the possible out of impossibilities. A tragic shooting at the age of nineteen left him paralyzed from the chest down. Art was always a means of expression for him. With limited use of his arms and hands, he resorted to painting with his mouth at the advice of a mentor (CBS Chicago, 2018.) The results were stunning. At age forty-two, he was painting a portrait for the president. He eventually established classes where he taught others to paint and to never give up, even through major challenges.

Sometimes the unexpected happens, our goals are redirected, and tragedy brings everything to a halt. However, through faith and determination, alternatives and new normals form. Though it does not always happen quickly, we someday find ourselves in a big picture, helping others make it through some of the same challenges that threatened our journey.

To the challenged, disappointed, and wounded, I have a message: keep going. There is a brush inside you that will navigate you through the detours, see you through strange lands, hold you tight in uncertainties, and give you experience to help others. Determination is a brush of faith, hope, and tenacity. You can do it!

Chapter 9

EXAMPLES OF BRUSHES IN RECENT HISTORY

H istoriography is an interesting concept. It asks the question: "What is history?" It is easy to think of history as "what appears in history books." However, what is in a book, film, or documentary is, at best, a depiction of actual history. Those who write these depictions do so based upon perspectives, biases, and selective input. So, one's historical account should never be considered an exhaustive full account of what actually took place.

Therefore, the following short depictions of history are not intended to be everything one needs to know about the subjects; they will serve as background information in order to see brushes at work in a historical context. We will delve into the lives of three individuals: George Washington Carver, Martin Luther King, Jr., and Diana Frances Spencer. Each section will start with relative historical information. Then I will suggest applications of the "brushes of life" concepts (brush, paint, big picture, socialization, needs, and determination). It will be fun! Let's go.

George Washington Carver

The beginning days of the life of this iconic man were tragic and, at the same time, incredible. George was born just shy of the slavery era around 1864 in Diamond, Missouri. His father died shortly before his birth. He, his mother, and older brother were slaves to the Carver family. The Carvers easily abandoned the idea of slavery soon after it was abolished (Bolden, 2008). One day, slave thieves from the South came by and stole George and his mother with the intent of selling them to Southern slave owners. They just missed his brother, who managed to escape. Mr. and Mrs. Carver hired help in order to find and retrieve George and his mother. The person they hired's name was Bentley. Though Bentley was skillful and experienced, he was only able to come back with baby George. George's mother was never seen again. The Carvers took care of baby George and his brother like their own. George was sickly and had to stay close to Mrs. Carver. Therefore, he learned things like cooking, sewing, and doing laundry (Moore, 1971). His brother, Jim, helped Mr. Carver with outside work. When George did get outside, he grew gardens, learned different types of plants, and studied ways to make gardens grow. He was so good at making plants grow, other neighbors came to him and asked for help.

George dreamed of going to school and learning more about plants and their growth. At age eleven, he struck out on his own and moved to the nearest school for blacks, which was eight miles away. There he found a black couple who took him in so that he could attend school. He called them Uncle Andy and Aunt Mariah. He also attended church with them. George learned a great deal about plant life at school. He learned everything his teachers could teach him and therefore needed to look for another school. He eventually moved to Fort Scott, Kansas, where he was hired by Mr. and Mrs. Payne as a cook. One day, some white men in Fort Scott killed a black man. This had a profound effect on George, and he eventually moved to another town, where he found another school for blacks. George made a living cooking and doing laundry for people. He moved from town to town attending schools. He was able to finally finish high school and apply for colleges. George was ecstatic when he received an acceptance letter from Highland College in Highland, Kansas. He used money he had saved to buy a train ticket. When he got to Highland, he found out that they did not accept black students. He was very disappointed and crushed. Feeling like he had come to a dead end, he continued to support himself by doing laundry.

One day, George heard about a college called Simpson College, which had one black student. He thought that perhaps they would accept another. He applied, and the college accepted him. George was an exceptional student, and his teachers poured into him. George eventually moved to Iowa State College and became a popular student there too. However, the laws of segregation did not allow him to eat in the dining room with the white students. Because of his race, he had to eat alone in a basement. He became the first black person to graduate from Iowa State. George eventually became a teacher at the college and contributed much to their science department.

One day, George got a letter from Booker T. Washington inviting him to come teach at a college for blacks called Tuskegee Institute. Though the college was limited in resources, George felt that this was a great opportunity to help other black people. He thought about the memorable events in his life that reflected the unfair treatment to black people. Going to Tuskegee was something he felt compelled to do, and he would work for little to no compensation. At the Tuskegee Institute, innovative solutions evolved from the needs of the area farmers. The main crop, cotton, had drained and depleted the soil of its nutrients. George knew that farmers needed to plant other crops and rotate their produce. He introduced them to other foods like sweet potatoes and peanuts, which made the soil rich for healthier crops. He also discovered many uses for these items so that they could be more in demand. His effort to help the farmers in his area not only led to hundreds of uses of the peanut but also brought a lot of attention to him and the college. He became a coveted speaker and an important voice in agriculture. He lived to receive many accolades, including his image on a United States postal stamp.

At the time of his death in 1943, he was helping to furnish the museum that would feature his important contributions. "President Franklin Delano Roosevelt dedicated a national monument in Missouri to George's memory; It was the first U.S national monument to honor an African American" (Mortensen, 2008, p. 22).

Brushes – What were the tools available to George Washington Carver that allowed him to make the impact he made? These tools were brushes and enabled him to paint such a masterpiece of success. What do you think? I may not name them all; however, I'll start with his education. His learning was a brush. The knowledge and concepts he was able to comprehend in his schooling enabled him to be of help to others. What about his experience as an African American? The cultural kindship he had with struggling black students and farmers enabled him to sympathize enough to find solutions. What about his ability to cook? Maybe you can think of more, but I'll stop there so I can go on to the next "brushes of life" concept.

Paint – So, what medium flowed with the brushes of education and culture in Carver's case? How about his laboratories?

He often synthesized his basic knowledge with challenges that needed solutions. Answers would all come together through his experimentations in his labs. At one time, he traveled around to farmers with a cart, bringing them information and support. Other media ("paint") included his lectures, presentations, and writings. He developed a repertoire of successes by these means.

Big Picture – The masterpiece was his forever uplift to humanity. His inventions, connections, and overcoming of barriers are some of the features of his mindboggling contributions.

Socialization – Carver's unique situation as a young child made him privy to an interest in the wonders of nature. Being small and sickly, the need for nurture kept him close to home and a masterful manager of his garden. It is probable that the care he received from Mrs. Carver informed his ability to care for the plant life he learned to nurture to good health.

Needs – Carver had a need for self-actualization. It led him to seek education and move several times as a young man.

His need to "give back" also led to his acceptance of professorship at an African American college where he would receive less wages.

Determination – There were many times in Carver's life where he had to use the brush of determination. The time that is most notable in my opinion is when he was turned down for college because of his race. It must have been devastating to him. However, he managed to keep existing and moving to the next opportunity. Eventually, other doors opened that allowed him to keep using his brushes, keep "painting," and finally begin putting together a masterpiece.

This is fun! Let's go to the next historical example.

Martin Luther King, Jr.

The legacy of Dr. King lives on, and we celebrate it afresh in street names, quoted speeches, and a national holiday. However, I suggest we pay attention to a few things from his childhood that set up a foundation for his eventual impact. We should first look at his grandfather, a noted minister of Ebenezer Baptist Church in Atlanta, Georgia, and a man who was involved in his community. Martin Luther King's mother, Alberta, grew up in a household where a passionate minister was the norm. It is no wonder that she accepted and married a hard-working young minister who studied under and admired her father (McKissack, 1984). Her husband, Mike King (later to become Martin King, Sr.), grew up having to fend for himself because of an alcoholic father. Mike's mother did everything she could for the family while cleaning for a banker. Mike, with a dream to one day own a two-story house like his mother's employer, struck out on his own at age fifteen. Mike was determined to succeed by working odd jobs at night and going to school by day. In eleven years, he finally earned his high school diploma. After marrying Alberta, he became the pastor of Ebenezer Church upon the passing of his father-in law. Alberta was an educator, and she and Mike instilled the importance of education into their three children. Their youngest child, Martin, Jr., took this to heart as he embarked upon first grade. There was one big problem, however. He could not attend school with his best friend, who was white. It was a teachable moment as his father reassured him that he was as good as anyone else. Though the color of his skin forbade him to attend school with his friend, he should realize that everyone was equal in God's eyes. Martin went on to soar academically and graduated from Booker T. Washington High School at age fifteen. At age nineteen, he graduated from Morehouse College with a degree in sociology. He received a Bachelor of Divinity degree from Crozer Theological Seminary two years later. At age twenty-six, he earned a Ph.D. from Boston University in systematic theology.

Fast-forward to the bus boycott that brought him to the forefront. He was a new minister in Montgomery, Alabama, and had recently moved there from Atlanta. When Rosa Parks, a well-respected hardworking seamstress in the African American community, was arrested for refusing to give up her bus seat for a white man, black ministers sprang into action. They looked for a leader and spokesperson to organize a bus boycott. Martin was reluctant but accepted the task after talking it over with his wife, Coretta.

Martin was calculating, motivating, eloquent, and able to bring people together. After the success of the bus boycott, his help and opinion were more in demand. Martin visited and spoke at black churches all across the South. He utilized the methods of Mahatma Gandhi to tailor his own peaceful protests. He led marches and sit-ins in the face of danger and adverse circumstances. He was jailed at least thirty times as he clashed with unfair Jim Crow laws. His relentless effort to bring justice to African Americans resulted in the honor of the nomination and receiving of a Nobel Peace Prize.

One of his most memorable speeches was in August of 1963, where he invited hundreds of people to join him at the National Mall in Washington D.C. There on the steps of the Lincoln Memorial, he voiced what many identify as the "I Have a Dream" speech. In it, he captured iconic and symbolic images embedded in the cultural songs and the common hope of the American dream.

History goes on to tell us that he was killed at age thirty-nine in Memphis, Tennessee, where he was planning a march supporting sanitation workers struggling with low wages. The irony of looking back at his heroic life from our modern-day perspective is we tend to think his support was strong among his own people. However, many African American leaders in his time were hesitant and critical of his progressive agenda to bring change. In that context, he often felt lonely in his pursuits and passions to carry out his convictions. Yet through physical danger, conflicting philosophies, and little support, he persevered.

Brushes – I am not sure if it is appropriate to try to numerate the brushes Dr. King used to make a lasting impact upon his generation and those to come. It seems an itemizing attempt would place limitations upon his toolbox for social justice. However, at the risk of trivializing his multiple talents, I will name a few. He had the ability to speak in both impromptu and formal settings. According to Maya Angelou, the finale of his "I Have a Dream" speech was a divergence from his notes. Yet it continues to be quoted by those who study his words. In addition to the brush of speaking, King's position as a minister worked to his advantage. Being a minister gave him a platform and avenue for reaching people, acceptance, and respect. In addition to the brush of his profession, he utilized the brush of education. His thirst for knowledge informed his pursuit for change and resulted in the acquisition of methodologies for peaceful protests and weighted ideas. We see this in another brush, the brush of writing as he referenced history and the Constitution to authenticate his conclusions.

Paint – If one of his brushes was his ability to write, then one of the mediums to an end result could be his book (*The Measure of Man*) or his "Letter from Birmingham Jail." His use of writing is even found in the quotes often associated with him, such as, "Violence is the language of the unheard," or, "Injustice anywhere is a threat to justice everywhere." These are the paints used by the brushes to stroke the eventual masterpiece. Other paints may be the organized marches like the one in Selma, Alabama, or the one on Washington or sit-ins at lunch counters where African Americans were not welcomed to sit. I hear you—"What about the bus," you say? Yes, the bus boycott was also definitely a good example as it was born from the brushes of intellect, speaking, and organizing to the outcome of more equality for African Americans on the city buses.

Big Picture– Equality becomes the painting. Not only equality, but also the maintaining of justice and equality becomes an important part of the picture. The "masterpiece" of the legacy of King is its tendency to be the crossroad of many perspectives looking for peace. His martyrdom seems to solidify his symbolic stand for non-violence. His commemorations often emphasize the importance of social justice, service, and help for the marginalized and uncounted.

Socialization – How could such a man so privy to education and a holder of three degrees feel enough empathy for the less fortunate to risk his own life helping them? The answer may emerge from his socialization. On both sides of his family, he had the heritage of looking out for others and those who struggled. His father knew what it meant to be without and to overcome with education and hard work. As a minister, Mike King understood how to vouch for those in need of encouragement. Martin Luther King, Jr.'s mother as a PK (preacher's kid) knew what it meant to give of herself. As an educator, she must have seen firsthand the value of pouring into the lives of others. Her children growing up in the reality of segregation must have given her valuable teachable moments in which she nourished the potential within them.

Needs – Martin must have had a need to reach self-actualization. When given the option to be silent or speak, he executed his need to be vocal and clearly stated where he stood. One of his quotes suggested this need when he said, "The ultimate tragedy is not the oppression and cruelty by the bad people but the silence over that by the good people" (Murphy, 2018).

Determination – King's "brush of determination" was evident in the words he spoke the night before he died. In front of a crowd of hundreds of people, he said:

> And then I got into Memphis. And some began to say the threats, or talk about the threats that were out. What would happen to me from some of our sick white brothers? Well, I don't know what will happen now. We've got some difficult days ahead. But it really doesn't matter with me now, because I've been to the mountaintop.

> And I don't mind. Like anybody, I would like to live a long life. Longevity has its place. But I'm not concerned about that now. I just want to do God's will. And He's allowed me to go up to the mountain. And I've looked over. And I've seen the Promised Land. I may not get there with you. But I want you to know tonight, that we, as a people, will get to the promised land! (CNN, 2018)

King's brush of determination took him past threats, set-backs, being misunderstood, imprisonments, and other obstacles. He made full use of this tool to affect the magnitude of his big picture.

The seemingly accelerated life of Dr. King has always been fascinating to me. It is interesting to delve into its wealth of information and align aspects of it to the concept of "brushes of life." I imagine there is a lot more we could find; however, that could be some other time. Meanwhile, let us go across the waters to look at another interesting life, that of a royal princess. Come on!

Princess Diana Frances Spencer

A British family gave birth to a little girl on July 1, 1961. The odds were against her immediately, considering her parents wanted a boy. She was their fourth attempt for a male. After their third baby girl died in miscarriage, Diana Frances Spencer entered their world. She knew early the feelings of disconnect and "not measuring up" though born in a family of privilege. Almost three years later, Diana's parents finally got their baby boy, who became the godson of Queen Elizabeth II.

Little Diana cherished her baby brother, and they grew close while their two older sisters lived abroad in boarding school (Labrecque, 2017). Like other wealthy children, Diana and her brother had nannies who helped care for them. Diana's father taught his children to be respectful to everyone and that people were equal and valuable, regardless of economic status.

Mr. Spencer was a "home body" and was content staying home reading on his "off days." Mrs. Spencer was adventurous, often bored, and wanted to explore the world (Labrecque, 2017). The two began to grow apart and finally separated when Diana was just six years old. Diana's mother moved away to London and saw Diana only on weekends. The marriage deteriorated into divorce in 1969, and this weighed heavily on Diana. The breakup of her parents, her inability to focus, and issues of disconnection became evident in her schoolwork. Though she was bright and intelligent, her grades were poor. Still, she was good at many other things, such as swimming, dancing, and playing piano.

One other quality emerged as Diana grew. She loved to take care of others. At one point, she and her friend faithfully visited an old woman who lived near their school. They would clean up, run errands for her, and make sure she was okay.

Diana also frequently visited the hospital for the mentally and physically disabled once a week. She had a special ability to care for those who needed support.

When Diana was almost fourteen, her grandfather died, and her father moved up in the royal line of succession to become the eighth Earl Spencer. Her family moved into a historic mansion known as the Althorp House, and Diana officially became Lady Diana. This ninety-room estate had been in their family for over 500 years.

When Diana was fifteen, she completed her boarding school studies. She scored poorly on her final exams and was not able to get into college. As an alternative, her parents sent her to "finishing school." There, young women learned how to be the wives of affluent and prominent husbands. Diana hated being in finishing school and convinced her parents to let her leave after only a few months.

When she returned, she got an apartment with a friend and a job as an assistant kindergarten teacher. She was exceptional in taking care of children, and many parents had no idea she was a part of the nobility. During this time, she met Charles, Prince of Wales and son of Queen Elizabeth. He was twelve years her senior, and they started talking at a cookout to which they were both invited. As their meeting increased, the media got wind of it and started following her. The media (paparazzi) even took pictures of her and her kindergarten students.

Diana and Charles were married on July 29, 1981. To their union were born two boys. As the boys grew, Diana knew she wanted her boys to grow up feeling accepted. She would often take them with her during their royal trips. She wanted them to experience life as regular kids and not feel isolated from society. Charles and Diana's marriage started to deteriorate, and they divorced when the boys were fourteen and eleven years of age.

Diana had been using her platform as a princess to bring awareness to the needs of others (Burrell, 2006). She traveled to different countries, encouraging others to donate to charities. Her leadership in showing empathy to those with challenges changed the thoughts of many. For example, she took photographs with AIDS patients and reminded people that it was okay to touch them. Diana often took her boys with her so that they could learn compassion for others. She also visited India and met Mother Teresa, whom she admired greatly. Mother Teresa let her visit all of the terminally ill patients.

After Diana's divorce from Prince Charles, she seemed to flourish in her newfound freedom and sense of purpose. She continued to travel the world visiting hospitals and homeless shelters. She visited Africa and brought attention to victims of land mine explosions. She also used the auctioning of her own clothing to raise money for AIDS and cancer patients.

Diana died tragically on August 30, 1997, when the car she was in lost control in a Paris tunnel as they tried to flee from paparazzi. She was thirty-six years old.

Brushes – Diana found something of interest early on, and she embraced it: that was the "idea of helping others." One could deduct that Diana was filling in a gap she missed as a child. Being able to pay attention to details and providing empathy became her interests and expertise. This brush may not be easily recognizable. It is not a profession, career, or typical skill; however, one can use it to create an outcome.

In addition to the "brush of helps," she used the brush of fashion. As she realized her influence and welcomed the opportunities designers had to offer, she ventured into looks never before seen on princesses. She seemed to represent the common woman and her right to be herself. Therefore, her clothing was the envy of the world, and she knowingly used it to help her charities.

Paint – The paint, of course, was the media in which she expressed herself. The charities, such as the AIDS Foundation, the Red Cross, and others, gave her the means by which she could attend to the needs of others. She also visited children's hospitals, homeless shelters, the Angola land mines victims' advocates, and taught kindergarten to spread this idea of caring.

Big Picture – Her masterpiece was just that – one of caring and the importance of paying attention to the needs of others. As her sons continue in her legacy, they too continue to raise awareness of humanitarian causes. This reputation and picture of empathy are often traced back to Diana.

Socialization – Diana's privileged environment as a child equipped her for her continual royalty as a princess. However, the ideas her father instilled in her helped her see all people as equals and worthy of comfort. Her own feelings of displacement informed her in her empathy for others and became a driving force in her work.

Needs – Therefore, her need for belonging assisted her understanding of "the need to belong" in others. When she touched AIDS patients, she provided them the chance to connect with society again and fulfill the need of inclusion.

In addition, she had a need to achieve self-actualization and be all she could be. As a teenager, she, no doubt, felt this could happen if she married a prince. After marrying at the age of twenty, a more mature Diana emerged in her thirties. The decision to depart from her marriage afforded her the opportunity to be herself and thereby be her best. (This is not an endorsement for divorce.) She put into play the brushes available and faithful to her and began making a difference where she could.

As a Pentecostal preacher, I cannot help but make a brief reference to the story of David right here. Diana was somewhat like David in achieving big things. David was too young to go to war. However, while taking his big brothers a "care package" from their dad, he overheard a giant bragging from the enemies' camp. David was appalled because everyone (including his brothers) were afraid to confront the giant. David, at that moment, signed up to go against this nine-foot, nine-inch man who was not only protected with heavy armor but who also had armor bearers on either side of him. When the captain of David's army found out about the scheduled duel, he offered David a complete uniform. David would have access to heavy armor, weapons, and any gear necessary for the fight. After David tried some of these things on, he decided not to use any of them. He used the tools with which he was familiar. David took off the heavy armor and went to the river and picked out five smooth stones for his slingshot. In his culture, boys learned to use slingshots so accurately they could hit flying creatures far away. When the duel started, David went right for the giant's face and sank a stone right into his unprotected forehead. This big, braggadocious man fell flat to the ground.

Diana was like David. She used the tools familiar to her. These included empathy, caring, fashions, and popularity. These stones (brushes) may have seemed insignificant, but with the right swing, she was able to knock down giants.

Determination – As a child, Diana used the brush of determination when she felt unconnected and displaced. She braved her way through the separation of parents and found her place. When her grades were not up to par, she moved forward with determination and landed upon a job as an assistant kindergarten teacher. It was a perfect place where she could put her caring into action.

One other obvious challenge for Diana was the spotlight which often infringed upon her privacy. This challenge ultimately caused her death. Paparazzi following her around and documenting her every move must have been crippling, especially when she needed time to herself. Rather than conceding to depression and despair, however, Diana figured a way to utilize the media and bring attention to her causes.

We could go on and on walking the halls of history finding lives in which we can apply the elements of the Brushes of Life (BOL). In each stop, we could probably dig deeper and find brushes, paints, and masterpieces not noticed before. However, these examples show that there is a definite pattern of using available tools to make a mark. Reflecting on the past gives power to the present. Insight during the present enables us to better plan for the future.

Chapter 10

The Start of Something Great

So, the world turned upside down within a matter of weeks during the COVID-19 crisis. All of us can probably remember where we were and what was happening when we realized everything had to shut down. It was humbling and scary at the same time. Out of it came many adjustments. "Business as usual" was lost forever. One of the changes I had to make was to be a pastor at a church where we could not meet regularly. One of the few solutions we implemented was for me to make a weekly video and upload it onto social media. Though I had recorded speaking to people many times, talking to a quiet camera was intimidating. I had to start and start again. Sometimes, my frustrations showed, and I made plenty of material for the bloopers clips. However, I began to notice that the more I started over, the more comfortable I was. There were at least one or two times when I thought I did a good job, and for some reason, I had to do it over. It may have been the pickup of a buzzing sound in the next room or an inaccurate focus of the camera. Whatever the problem, I was forced a couple of times to rerecord. When that happened, I discovered that my last recording would feel more natural and come out better. I was beginning to realize that practice and repetition were my friends. Though it was sometimes a pain, practicing was a good thing.

Likewise, we get better with the tools we use if we continue to use them. It may sound basic, but practicing allows us to become better at expressing what we want to say. I can always tell when a middle-schooler has been drawing a lot. There is something about his/her line quality. There is a flair of confidence in rendering. It is deliberate, intentional, and bold because the young artist has been there before through practice. I have seen it happen. Then someone walks by the young artist and says, "Wow! He/she can really draw!" That rings true, and one often thinks it is only due to gifts and artistic genes. Some of that may be true, but one must remember the power of practice. The more you do, the better you do. The more you use your brush, the better you become and the more likely you are to accomplish the masterpiece.

That being said, let us look at what motivates us to practice. We are more likely to practice those things in which we have an interest. When a new musician takes an interest in an instrument, the first notes are crude, flat, and imperfect. There have been parents who wondered if they made the right decision purchasing that drum set for Christmas! However, bit by bit, the rehearsal becomes tolerable. Soon, the music is enjoyable, and guests are welcomed to listen in. It was interest coupled with encouragement that motivated the new musician into skillful expressions.

Therefore, one must make room and allowance for practicing. It is good when one's interest motivates and initiates the use of tools. Other factors will keep the practicing going. These include encouragement, feelings of accomplishment, systematic and random reinforcements, and scheduled time for rehearsal. Though these applications sound musical, the concept is true for any tool of preference. It could be growing plants, as in the case of George Washington Carver, or public speaking, as in the case of Martin Luther King, Jr. It may be caring for people, as in the case of Princess Diana. Whatever the brush, when repetition is involved, its handling becomes more efficient, bold, and intentional.

One other item fuels practice, and that is passion. Passion takes interest to another level. Where there is an intense desire to do, practice becomes less cumbersome. This is why it may be helpful to find one's passion. When hosting interns in my art classroom, I have an option of providing them with everything to teach or allowing them to teach from their passions. I always find that when I encourage these future teachers to address the curriculum with some medium or style meaningful to them, their art lesson takes on life. There is something about teaching from one's passion. It brings out the best in the teacher, and students learn more. The teacher is willing to put in time for preparation. Creativity flows, and the excitement is contagious. This is the power of passion.

Author Elizabeth Gilbert (2015) challenges the pursuit of passion. She suggests that persons who are looking for their purpose in life may become anxious in an attempt to identify passions. Gilbert, therefore, recommends following one's curiosities. She likens following curiosity to the actions of a hummingbird. A hummingbird goes from plant to plant, spreading pollen and substances that would benefit the entire area. If we, like the hummingbird, follow our curiosities, over time, we will positively affect a wide range of components impacted by our pursuits. The idea is to relax and satisfy the need to discover and know more. As we do this, we provide more positive energy to our surroundings, and, eventually, we stumble upon our passions and purpose.

It is important we have some fun. Not only is the destination significant, but the journey is also important. This is what I call "laughing in the kitchen." I know this sounds funny, but bear with me. I love to hear laughter in the kitchen. When I go to a restaurant or a fast food place, anytime I hear workers laughing as they do their work, I know they have a good relationship, and the morale is healthy. They are in harmony as they accomplish their goals. No doubt, they have a quota to meet. There must be a time goal from the moment an order comes in until the time the food is in the hand of the customer. As important as these goals are, it is just as important to have a good atmosphere and enjoy the process. When I hear laughing in the kitchen, as a customer, my food tastes better. There is just something attractive about people having fun.

As we do what we do, find our purpose, and satisfy our curiosities, we should remember to "laugh in the kitchen." When one is too serious, critical, mean, and suspicious, The Big Picture is tainted. Therefore, lighten up, have some fun, and enjoy what you do. Others will appreciate the atmosphere.

Carol Dweck (2006) refers to this type of mindset when suggesting the advantages of a learning mentality. The growth mindset is one that is not marked by anxiety because of perfectionistic mandates. One with a growth mindset is driven by an attitude of improvement. On the other hand, a fixed mindset is about winning and being "right." This makes us afraid to extend ourselves to explore and try new things. For example, when learning to skate, a person needs to have a growth mindset. This will allow the person to be open enough to make mistakes, fall a few times, and progress to new things. However, if the person has a fixed mindset, they are more likely to go only as far as they can do perfectly and thereby miss an opportunity to improve.

A growth mentality, therefore, can be very advantageous when putting the brushes of life to use. Being willing to learn, have fun, discover, and enjoy the process makes reaching the masterpiece an exhilarating experience. One is likely to repeat the experience over and over, rehearsing one's way into a greater level of expertise. The bottom line is…"have fun."

Realize that life's brushes, though seemingly of little value, are the start of something great. Over time, through dedication, following curiosity, and having a little fun, we make it to a big picture. Greatness is bound to happen. A masterpiece is in the making. Enjoy yourself!

Chapter 11

MY BRUSHES OF LIFE

Sometimes I have a little fun with my students when teaching them about cropping and the frame of reference. I would take an image, preferably one with which they are familiar, and zoom in on one particular part. I would zoom in close enough so that the section takes on its own character. I would show this cropped version without them knowing what the complete picture is. I would allow them time to guess and identify the painting to which the crop belongs. The answers are surprising; they see alien ships, mechanical parts, upside-down faces, and all kinds of images they can imagine. When I show them The Big Picture, there is often a reaction all over the room ranging from, "I knew it!" to, "I never would have

guessed it." As they do several of these, they began to understand the dynamics of the full picture vs. its components.

If you noticed my reference to The Big Picture, you may
realize where I am going with this. Sometimes as we "work
our brushes" and carry out our lives, we are working with the
zoomed-in image. We only see up close, and what we see takes
on a character of its own. We cannot see the forest (as the
cliché goes) because we are so close to the trees. Therefore,
we get lost in what we do, even bogged down, and sometimes
despairingly depressed because we are overwhelmed with rou-
tine and ritual. What we need at that point is a little zooming
out time. Often times when an artist steps back and sees
the entire picture, he/she can envision how all things come
together. The artist may take the opportunity to adjust pro-
portions and redistribute colors.

This is applicable to our awareness of the "brushes of life."
We should take the opportunity to hold our heads up, think
about big things, and see where our brushes are taking us.
Zooming out informs us, allows us to regain our bearings, and
eventually inspires us to zoom back in and work harder. Take
a moment and realize, "I'm working on something big."

This reminds me of the story of three construction workers. A person walked up to one and asked, "What are you doing?"

The worker replied, "I'm laying these bricks."

The person stepped up to the second worker and asked, "What are you doing?"

The second person replied, "I'm building this wall."

The inquisitive person asked the last worker, "What are you doing?"

The third worker said, "I'm building a cathedral!"

The third worker clearly had taken some time to zoom out. Zooming out gave him a bigger perspective as he zoomed in. The worker realized more the "value of his work."

The "value of your brush" is worth repeating. We should let no one (including ourselves) devalue our brushes. Unfortunately, we deem some professions as superior to others. This may be due to the income attached to certain jobs. However, regardless of what the pay, your brush is priceless. Whether you are an Uber driver, ER doctor, musician, grocery bagger, defense lawyer, meter reader, dog trainer, or carnival worker, what you do is valuable. The tool contributes to a big picture. Relax and enjoy the process. Do not get jealous or feel inferior to anyone else. Know that the brush is secondary to the masterpiece. Very few people who walk into the Louvre in Paris, France, and gaze upon the Mona Lisa ask to see the brush Leonardo da Vinci used. He could have used a stick with a piece of cloth on the end, a palette knife, or a cotton ball. The most important thing is the painting of the woman whose eyes follow us across the room. Do not be disheartened by the expense of the tool. Never "discount" it. It is what it is because of where it is going. Keep painting.

In addition to "brushes of life" awareness, remember not to limit oneself. It is okay to have plenty of brushes or change brushes at different points in life. It is okay to rethink, redraw, correct, and refine our brushes and our pictures. Make sure that the determination brush sees us through difficult roadblocks. Let our needs drive us to the fulfillment of our dreams. Let the socialization of familiarity cause us to be curious about the unfamiliar. Bring your gifts to the table and respect the gifts of others. Realize that we all have something to offer and dispel your own insecurities by being an advocate for the success of others. This way, we will all win and find ourselves in the gallery of masterpieces.

I said in the beginning that even this book can be a brush. Use it as a tool, a mechanism, and an instrument by which you discover new ideas, explore possibilities, and arrive at The Big Picture. Let it inform you when your creativity is at a standstill. This book does not contain all the answers. It is just an argument for a way to look at the complexities of life. Take what works for you and discard what doesn't. Build upon what matters. Continue to "brush away." And someday, the picture will become clear so that you and others can celebrate it. You can do this!

I have to end with this appropriate scripture from the Bible (I told you I am a minister!) It is Ephesians 2:10. It reads, "For we are his workmanship, created in Christ Jesus unto good works, which God hath before ordained that we should walk in them." It appears this scripture is implying that our brushes are God-given. He purposed us to walk in them and use them to do good works. When we follow through, we will find that the Creator is creating a masterpiece through us. We are His workmanship, and we have the privilege to be a part of His fabulous gallery.

ABOUT THE AUTHOR

Dr. Donald Elisha Sheppard has been the pastor of Watson Temple Institutional Church of God in Christ in Tallahassee, Florida, for twenty-two years. Dr. Sheppard was a design artist for nine years and has taught middle school art for over twenty-six years.

He has a Bachelor of Fine Arts degree from the Columbus College of Art and Design (Columbus, Ohio) and both masters and Ph.D. degrees from Florida State University in art education.

Dr. Sheppard has been married to Sarah Rivers Sheppard for thirty-three years. They have one adult daughter, Donarah.

References

Bolden, T. (2008). George Washington Carver. Abram Books for Young Readers. New York.

Burrell, P. (2006). The Way We Were: Remembering Diana. HarperCollins Publishers. New York, NY

Call, J. (2018, February 21). Invoking the memory of their lost classmates, Parkland students urge legislative action on guns. *Tallahassee Democrat*. Retrieved July 12, 2020 from https://www.tallahassee.com/story/news/2018/02/21/invoking-memory-their-lost-classmates-stoneman-douglas-high-school-students-urge-legislators-act-gun/360854002/

Callan, K. (1997). Biography, Vincent Van Gogh: A Stroke of Genius. A&E Television Networks. New York, NY.

CBS Chicago (2018, December 27). Shooting Victim Learns To Paint With His Mouth, Finds Love. Retrieved July 12, 2020 from https://youtu.be/qtyfO3zkc1w

CNN (2018, April 4). Here is the speech Martin Luther King Jr. gave the night before he died. Retrieved April 27, 2021 from https://www.cnn.com/2018/04/04/us/martin-luther-king-jr-mountaintop-speech-trnd

Dobson, B. (2017, February 17). Greg Grady's influence after 33 years of working with the city's youth will be missed. *Tallahassee Democrat*. Retrieved July 12, 2020, https://www.tallahassee.com/story/opinion/2017/02/17/greg-gradys-influence-after-33-years-working-citys-youth-missed/98025200/

Dweck, C. S. (2006). Mindset: The New Psychology of Success. Ballantine Books. New York.

Efland, A., 1990. A history of art education: Intellectual and social currents in teaching the visual arts. Teachers College Press. New York, NY.

Gardner, H. (1985). *Frames of Mind*. New York: Basic Books.

Gardner, H. (1999). *Intelligence reframed: Multiple intelligences for the 21st century*. New York: Basic Books.

Gilbert, E. (2015, November 6). Elizabeth Gilbert: Don't Chase Your Passion And Maybe You'll Find It. OWN. Retrieved July 12, 2020, https://www.youtube.com/watch?v=Z_PSUskgiZU

Harris, M. & Chen, J. (2018). Michelle Obama meets 2-year-old who admired her portrait — and dances with her! Today. Retrieved July 12, 2020 from https://www.today.com/parents/michelle-obama-meets-2-year-old-who-looked-portrait-awe-t124575

Labrecque, E. (2017). Who Was Princess Diana? Grosser & Dunlap, Penguin Random House. New York, NY

Maslow, A. H. (1943). "A theory of human motivation" *Psychological Review*. 50(4): 370-96

McKissack, P. (1984). Martin Luther King, Jr.: A Man to Remember. Children's Press. Chicago

Moore, E. (1971). The Story of George Washington Carver. Scholastic, Inc. New York.

Mortensen, L. (2008). George Washington Carver: Teacher, Scientist, and Inventor. Picture Window Books. Minneapolis, Minnesota

Murphy, B. (2018, January 12). "17 Inspirational Quotes From Martin Luther King Jr. About Speaking Up When It Matters." Inc. Retrieved April 28, 2021 from https://www.inc.com/bill-murphy-jr/17-inspirational-quotes-by-martin-luther-king-jr-about-speaking-up-when-it-matters.html

Robertson, I. (1977). Sociology. Worth Publishers, Inc. New York, N.Y.

Stone, I. (1961). The Agony and the Ecstasy. Doubleday. Garden City, N. Y.

Tada, J. E. (2001). Joni: An Unforgettable Story. Zondervan. Grand Rapids, Michigan

TheEllenShow (2019, September 20). Retrieved July 12, 2020 from https://www.youtube.com/watch?v=QntBkDFkiuY

The Official Steve Harvey (2018, October 15). Follow Your Gift, Not Your Passion. Retrieved July 12, 2020. https://www.youtube.com/watch?v=3x3rEg2qvcQ